IMAGES
of America

WINTHROP

WELCOME TO WINTHROP, C. THE 1940S. The fire department leads a patriotic celebration in one of the many parades held on Main Street.

IMAGES
of America

WINTHROP

David S. Cook

ARCADIA
PUBLISHING

Published by Arcadia Publishing
Charleston, South Carolina

Library of Congress Catalog Card Number: 2003103769

For all general information contact Arcadia Publishing at:
Telephone 843-853-2070
Fax 843-853-0044
E-mail sales@arcadiapublishing.com
For customer service and orders:
Toll-Free 1-888-313-2665

Visit us on the Internet at www.arcadiapublishing.com

THE BICENTENNIAL PARADE, 1971. One of many memorable moments for the town of Winthrop was its bicentennial parade. Holding the banner, as the celebrants march east on Main Street, are Jody Sylvester, on the left, and Judy Ward, on the right. The wet pavement and overcast skies did not slow anyone down.

CONTENTS

ACKNOWLEDGMENTS

The photographs used in this book, with very few exceptions, come from the collections of Fred Rand and Roland LaVallee, to whom I dedicate this work.

Fred Rand was a tireless student of Winthrop's history, a collector of its memorabilia, and a source of information. His collection comprises photographs that he himself took or collected and many that were formerly owned by Charlie Loon. Before his death, Rand gave his collection to Roland LaVallee.

Roland LaVallee grew up in town and, after World War II, settled down in Winthrop. He became a photographer for the *Kennebec Journal* and has undoubtedly taken more pictures of Winthrop happenings than anyone else has. His photographs number well into the thousands. They depict school functions, club doings, and everything else that needed recording.

LaVallee gave his entire collection, including Rand's photographs, to the town a few years ago. Lisa Gilliam, town clerk, has been instrumental in affording me access to the collection and has my thanks.

Also, my thanks go to Also Russ and Kaye Riggs, who provided some postcards that I used in the book.

INTRODUCTION

People have lived in the Winthrop region for over 10,000 years. Native Americans left the first faint archaeological footprints along the banks of streams, islands, and outlets and inlets of lakes in the Cobbosseecontee watershed in the Kennebec Basin. The waterways of Maine create an aquatic highway. With canoes, the lakes and ponds are easily accessible, and, where necessary, portages, or as we say in Maine, "carries," can be made past a set of falls or to reach the headwaters of a different watershed. Carries were memorable places, as were the campsites and spots where hunting and fishing was good. Camps were often made on carry trails, where one might meet travelers, perhaps friends, passing through.

The little stream that plunges 50 feet in the quarter-mile run from Lake Maranacook to Lake Annabessacook was one such a memorable place. Here generations of Native Americans camped to fish for salmon or sturgeon. They carried their canoes past the falls; the lakes were links in a large network of prehistoric canoe routes. Those who resided in the region knew the value of this place.

Certainly, Native Americans had a name for the stream and the distinctive falls thousands of years before white men first saw the place or calculated the power of the falls. Properly harnessed by dams and geared into waterwheels, nature's power would be turned back on itself by these new arrivals, who used it to cut the trees into lumber and grind their grain into flour. Europeans arrived on the Kennebec River in the 17th century, bringing diseases, animals, and European wars to the maritime peninsula that Maine occupies with Quebec and New Brunswick. These factors combined to nearly extirpate the Native American people.

In the 18th century, the Kennebec region wound up in the hands of powerful men whose base was Massachusetts. In the 1760s, at the end of the French and Indian War, interior Maine became safe for Englishmen for the first time. The value of the land increased, creating a peace dividend for Massachusetts moguls named Hallowell, Gardiner, Bowdoin, Vassal, and Pitt, collectively known as the Kennebec Proprietors. Today, these names all denote Kennebec Valley towns to which the early settlers modestly attached their names. The vast woods of Maine was their main chance. Hard times in Massachusetts were a good time to offer easy terms to anyone who wanted to start over in "the eastern quarter."

The proprietors advertised their offerings and, by a variety of methods, sold land to would-be pioneers. In 1763, an agent of the Kennebec Proprietors passed through and later surveyed the region that lay then in Lincoln County, District of Maine of Massachusetts. In 1765, Winthrop's first settlers, Timothy and Sibella Foster, came to the west shore of Cobbosseecontee with their 10 children. Timothy Foster purchased a rude cabin and already-planted fields from a hunter and trapper named Samuel Scott, the agent for the Kennebec Proprietors who had made improvements and even planted a garden earlier in the summer on what is now Welsh's Point.

In a typical American frontier episode, Foster and Scott wound up in court. Scott claimed that Foster, on two different occasions in August and September 1765, "with force of arms broke and entered the plaintiff's Close and carried away ten Bushels of Potatoes, and ten bushels of Turnips, . . . and carried away twenty Pound weight of pork of theft, ten pounds Weight of beef and Quarter of a hundred of Bread . . . and carried away ten tons of meadow hay . . . and other enormities." Ten children do require a lot of food, and we do not know the terms of their agreement in the first place, but the Maine frontier was a place where one could, as many did, get swindled.

The court at Pownalborough turned the case over to three estimable locals as referees, who decided for Scott but reduced his award from £60 to £40 "lawful money" and £17 for court costs. There is no record that Foster paid, nor did he spend any time in jail. Soon, he was back home by the lake, and in 1766, he and Sibella welcomed their 11th child, a boy they named Steven.

Soon, others came and "let light into the swamp," laboriously clearing fields by removing trees, stumps, and rocks. Most survived those first lean years in Pond Town (Winthrop's early name). In the 19th century, Winthrop was described as a "thrifty agriculture town" known for fine horses, great apple crops, and a beautiful natural setting. Situated in southwestern Kennebec County 10 miles west of Augusta, Winthrop contains or borders eight lakes and ponds. The land is made up of both rolling hills and large expanses of good agricultural tracts. From Townhouse Hill, the high point on Metcalf Road, one can see the hills of Dixmont west of the Penobscot River, and to the west part of the White Mountains are clearly visible. Mount Pisgah, an 800-foot high hill, rises through the western portion of the town and also affords wonderful views of south central Maine.

Throughout the 19th century, agriculture was a main pursuit in the area. Dr. Ezekial Holmes, a Bowdoin College-trained doctor whose health kept him from practicing medicine, settled in Winthrop in the 1830s. He edited one of the first agricultural journals in the United States, *The Maine Farmer*. Besides having a farm on Mount Pisgah, "Doc" Holmes also had a house in the village. Holmes did more than any other person to introduce better farming methods and better breeds of livestock to Maine's hardworking and often hard-pressed farmers. Today, Holmes is known as "the Father of Maine Agriculture." A plaque honoring his contributions and a building named for him can be found at the University of Maine at Orono, an institution he helped to create.

Manufacturing played an ever increasing role from the early days, because of the many sources of waterpower found here. In 1766, John Chandler built a sawmill and, a year later, a gristmill across the outflow of Lake Maranacook. In return for his "sweat equity," the Kennebec Proprietors granted him a 400-acre lot that extended from Mill Stream east to the Narrows Ponds. His mills would encourage others to come, and they would have to pay for their lots.

Winthrop was incorporated in 1771 as Maine's 23rd town. Situated 10 miles from tidewater at Hallowell, it was the state's first town that was not on navigable water. Before Chandler built his mills, men had to carry their grain back and forth between Winthrop and Hallowell over a rude footpath. The burden was lighter on the return leg, because Gardiner took his pay in grain. Often the trip took more than one day. In 1767, when word came that the millstones had arrived from Massachusetts at the Hook (a section of Hallowell), Winthrop's entire male population turned out and, for nearly a week, struggled to bring the stones over hills and through swamps to a waterfall on a small stream that other people had once named and known.

Considerable manufacturing has been done in Winthrop ever since that time. By 1881, a woolen factory in the village was producing $150,000 worth of goods per year, and the gristmills ground over 12,000 bushels of all kinds of grain annually. There were bark and fulling mills and a sawmill that produced 200,000 feet of lumber a year. A cotton factory made yarn and lines, and there was a foundry and a machine shop. Whitman's Agricultural Tool Manufactory turned out cider mills, as well as horse rakes, hand rakes, and planing, threshing, and winnowing machines, to the value of nearly $100,000 yearly.

Elsewhere in Winthrop during the late 19th century, there were several small mills and a tannery. At Baileyville, in the eastern part of town, there was a large oilcloth factory run by the Bailey family. In East Winthrop, located in the northeastern part of the town and bordered on the south by the Cobbosseecontee, there was a prosperous village in its own right. When dammed, Meadow Brook, a small stream, was sufficient for an early potash factory and a tannery. The northern part of town, where the Metcalf neighborhood is located, was not on falling water, but it was an important place, an early center of the community. The hills were cleared and farmed for many years. Now the fields are covered with woods for the most part, but their traces are left in the stone walls that today only partially and ineffectively partition the woods themselves.

All of these places are home to a new generation of people, and all of these old pictures are but a poor glimpse of what has gone before.

One

MAIN STREET

THE VILLAGE, LOOKING EAST, 1903. Royal Street runs diagonally across the lower part of this image, which shows the neighborhood enjoying an August day 100 years ago. The large apartment block, at the left, was owned by Mr. Gilley. In the middle background, along Main Street, are the Winthrop Mill complex, called Carlton Woolen for the last 50 years, and the town hall. Houses and farms are visible on the way up Hinds Hill on the Augusta Road.

MAIN STREET, LOOKING EAST, C. 1920. Winthrop's business section contained many buildings that have since been torn down. The first four businesses on the left closed long ago, and the other three buildings were demolished. A large two-story building, later Wilson's Dollar Stores, was moved back several hundred feet in the 1980s. Note the four modes of transportation: the automobile, the bicycle, the trolley track, and the horse-drawn wagon in front of the drugstore.

MAIN STREET, LOOKING EAST, C. 1900. This earlier view also looks east. The gasoline signs advertise a relatively new product that spelled the demise of the horse-drawn era at the dawn of the 20th century. The four-story brick Pennimen Block, on the right, and the structure to the left of it, then housing Jackson's Drug Store, are the only buildings pictured that still stand on that side of the street. The Pennimen Block is now known as 48 Main Street.

MAIN STREET, LATE WINTER, C. 1890. This horse-drawn sled, traveling west on an unpaved street, will encounter worse conditions than this when mud season sets in with the spring thaw.

THE BLIZZARD OF 1952. This little dusting is well remembered by many people, and not just those in Winthrop. The sun has just broken through, and the town has started digging out. Little has changed in the 60 years that divide this image from the one above, except for the horse and the pavement beneath the plowed street.

OLD HOME WEEK, 1908. The gala atmosphere of this view looking east along Main Street is only one of scores of such events for which the community has taken to the streets for well over 100 years. Winthrop's notable esprit is on display, and many people still faithfully respond, as is evident in many of the past parades.

SMOKING RUINS ALONG MILL STREAM, C. 1890. The reason Winthrop village is nestled between two large lakes, Maranacook to the north and Annabessacook on the south, is this little stream. In less than half a mile, the stream descends 50 feet. It provided waterpower for mills beginning in 1767. Shown is the aftermath of a fire that damaged the lumberyard on the left and another facility. Over the years there were many fires in the mills along the stream. In this view looking north, the top of the Pennimen Block is visible in the distance to the right of center.

THE MILL DAM, MECHANICS ROW, C. 1890. This small dam, one of many built on Mill Stream over the last 235 years, runs out from the mills, which were built completely over the stream. Carlton Woolen closed forever in 2002, most probably ending manufacturing on this historic "mill privilege."

THE BENJAMIN HOUSE, MAIN STREET. This house was owned by Capt. Samuel Benjamin, who came to Winthrop in 1806. He purchased a small lot from Winthrop's pioneer mill builder, John Chandler, and he commenced making furniture. Born into a noteworthy Livermore family in September 1786, Benjamin served in the local militia. The house, still remembered, was torn down in the 20th century to make way for a bank.

MAIN STREET, SOUTH SIDE, C. 1900. The Winthrop Bakery was sold by E.W. Morris in 1901 to Mr. Boardman, the man on the far right. Boardman sold it to Edward Loughton, who eventually sold it to Lennie McNamara. McNamara ran it for many years and eventually started a restaurant that operated until the 1960s.

HIGH WATER ON MAIN STREET, C. 1900. This is not a strange sight to contemporary residents of Winthrop. In times of extreme precipitation, Mill Stream, which runs as seen here from right to left under the road and behind the barrels, comes over the way and provides a problem for pedestrians. This photograph offers a good view of the north side of the street. The five structures to the right of the four-story Pennimen Block have been gone for many years.

THREE CITIZENS, C. 1900. This dapper trio sits on Main Street, enjoying a conversation. Main Street is still a place where people bump into each other and chat before hurrying along their way. In earlier times men would commonly roost along the street and have "a good chew" over important items of the day. The granite posts pictured here now can be found at the bottom of Mill Stream just above the bridge.

TWO BUSINESSMEN, C. 1915. This apothecary was run by F.S. Jackson in 1918. Besides serving as a Rexall drugstore, the place was also the waiting room for the Lewiston, Augusta, and Winthrop Railway Company, better known as the trolley. A trip to Augusta took an hour and cost a quarter.

MILL WORKERS, NOVEMBER 23, 1893. The crew at the Winthrop Mills turns out for a group photograph. Well over 100 people were employed at the Winthrop Mills. Their ages ranged from the very young upward.

THE WINTHROP MILLS, C. 1920. Built on the site of John Chandler's sawmill and gristmill, this facility employed generations of area residents. Many children were raised on the living their parents made in this mill, natives and immigrants alike.

16

THE WINTHROP MILLS, NOVEMBER 23, 1893. This view features the crew and the tower. Most certainly, the 100 or so people pictured in this 110-year-old photograph have "crossed the dark river" by now, but do their shades still walk the old mill grounds?

A WORKSHOP, INTERIOR VIEW, C. 1915. These men, probably tinsmiths in a Main Street establishment, work with sheet metal. Note the overalls that three of them are wearing. The man in the center wearing trousers with soiled knees sports a tie underneath his jacket, indicating that he is probably in charge. In 1918, Winthrop had two hardware and tinware specialists: H.W. Stevens and J.H. McElroy.

ELM REMOVAL, MAIN STREET, 1969. One of the major changes in many small towns in the 1950s and 1960s was the loss, through storm or disease, of the large shade trees that had been set out 80 to 100 years before.

MAIN STREET, LOOKING WEST, C. 1949. The elm trees are prominent on the horizon. The elms once grew along most of the streets in town. Not only the trees but also some buildings that were familiar to generations disappeared over the next several decades.

THE DEMOLITION OF HASKELL'S SHOE STORE, JUNE 15, 1967. This old building was taken down to make way for another. In years past it was a harness shop, and Dr. Albert French had a dentist's office upstairs.

THE LEWISTON, GREENE, AND MONMOUTH TELEPHONE OFFICE. Many people remember going to this office to pay their telephone bills. The building was removed when a bank was built. Today, the space is occupied by the Key Bank.

THE TELEPHONE OFFICE'S LAST DAY, C. 1970. The post-and-beam construction and method of roof framing indicate that the old office building was constructed early in the 19th century.

DEMOLISHED FOR PARKING. In this view looking northwest, Haskell's small shoe store and Depositor's Trust are prominent. Haskell's has since been removed.

THE GEM THEATER, THE 1930S. The Gem Theater was built from the old Universalist church, which had stood on Main Street since 1868. The automobile reveals the period in which this photograph was taken.

THE NEW GEM, THE 1940S. The replacement for the old Gem, which burned in 1944, was a modern theater for its time. However, by the 1960s, such small businesses were competing in a losing economic battle with larger venues that had multiple screens and with much-improved television.

THE A & P SUPERMARKET, THE 1960s. This building replaced the Gem Theater. It was designed specifically for the Great Atlantic and Pacific Tea Company (A & P). Many A & P stores were built in small towns across the nation. The A & P in Winthrop lasted until the 1970s. Today, this is the location of the Winthrop House of Pizza.

WALTON'S GARAGE, THE 1930s. Art Walton, shown on the left wearing a tie, operated this garage on Union Street for a time during the 1930s. Pictured here with Walton are the mechanics and the bookkeeper.

THE GULL THEATER, 1952. The Gull Theater used the same building as Walton's Garage, on Union Street. The Gull is pictured between two Main Street buildings after the big snowstorm of 1952.

UNION STREET, WEST SIDE, THE 1950S. The Pond Town Tavern, Bruneau's Market, and Abelli's Fruit Store occupied buildings that are now gone. Only Lorette's Barber Shop and the two-story brick building on the corner of Union and Elm Streets still stand today.

WINTHROP'S FIRST LETTER CARRIER. Sid Nelson was the first mailman to deliver mail to townspeople. Pictured here during the 1940s, he was well known to residents. Note his well-pressed uniform and neat appearance.

ABELLI'S FRUIT STORE, C. 1938. Rose Abelli stands in front of the family store on Main Street before World War II. The terrier at her side looks suspiciously at the viewer. The man on the left is engaged in conversation.

HANNAFORD'S DRUGSTORE, C. 1948. Hannaford's was in business on Main Street for many years, with a pharmacy and newsstand at several locations. Such small pharmacies no longer exist in Winthrop, having been supplanted by large chain stores.

UNION STREET, WEST SIDE, C. 1965. The Pond Town Tavern, later known as the Paddock and now as Barney's Sports Bar, has moved to the east side of the street, and two of the buildings visible in the lower picture on page 23 are gone. Since this photograph was taken *c.* 1965, more changes have occurred.

MACNAMARA'S BAKERY, C. 1940. This winter view shows MacNamara's Bakery and Joe's Barbershop, on the right, operated by Joe Routhier. These buildings are now gone. For years, Smith's Mobil Station, now Park's Auto Repair, stood to the left just out of sight. Note the used cars for sale.

THE HOSE HOUSE, C. 1935. The Payson Tucker Hose Company, Winthrop's fire department, used this Union Street building for a number of years. The building was occupied by the Paddock establishment after the fire company moved. Today, it is the site of Barney's Sports Bar.

THE WINTHROP FIRE DEPARTMENT, THE 1950S. The fire chief stands in front of the new facility. Note the array of equipment, which over the years was used to save many buildings.

THE WINTHROP FIRE DEPARTMENT, THE 1960S. The new fire truck, on the right, looks more efficient than the older version. In any fire department, the age of the trucks often spans a number of years. Expensive to purchase, the vehicles today are being designed with capabilities that go beyond firefighting.

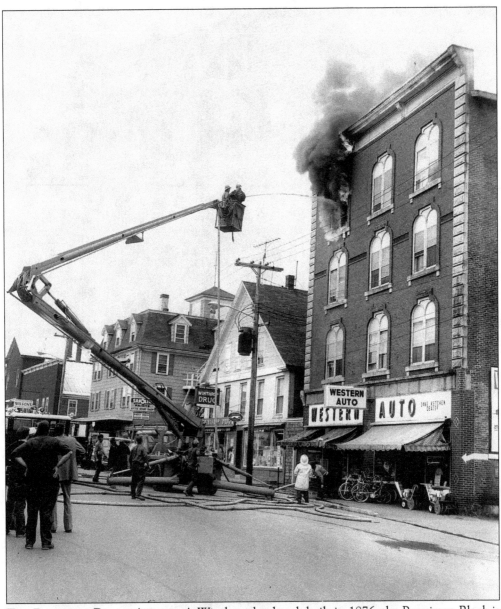

THE PENNIMEN BLOCK ABLAZE. A Winthrop landmark built in 1876, the Pennimen Block is shown with Winthrop firefighters directing water into the top floor. Fortunately, the fire did not destroy this important building. Reconditioned in 2000–2002, the Pennimen Block is in fine shape today.

THE WINTHROP HOUSE, C. 1920. This Winthrop landmark was built in 1800 by Capt. Barney Haskell. Over many years it was enlarged and remodeled. In past times it was known as the Winthrop Hotel and the Hotel Maine.

REMODELING THE WINTHROP HOUSE, THE 1950S. The hotel went through a series of renovations as the building was adapted to various uses. For example, the telephone company had its offices on the third floor before World War I.

THE HOTEL ON FIRE, 1985. A 1985 fire spelled the end for this old hotel, on the corner of Main and Union Streets. How many volumes could the stories of such a place fill? Today, the site holds a small park with benches and parking spaces.

THE NORCROSS GARAGE, THE 1920S. Pictured in front of the Norcross Garage, on Main Street, are members of the garage crew. Note the sale information in the window and the amounts that a buyer could save per purchase. Here, cars were bought, sold, traded, and fixed. In an adjoining building, a taxidermist plied his trade.

MAPLE CEMETERY, MAIN STREET. The land for this burying ground was donated to the town by Gideon Lambert and John Chandler, two pioneers of the town. The Chandler family plot is the first on the left beyond the cemetery entrance. The Lamberts are buried along the north side by the fence standing near the land they cleared and farmed. The large trees shown here have been removed. One of the felled elms had over 140 growth rings visible on its stump.

THE WINTHROP SCHOOL AND THE METHODIST CHURCH, C. 1900. The schoolhouse, on the left, served until 1910, when the high school was moved to Union Street. The old school has long since been removed; today, the space is used by a Keneco gas station. Enlarged several times, the Methodist church, on the right, is still in use.

Two

AROUND TOWN

THE BICENTENNIAL SEAL. This seal was designed in 1971 for Winthrop's bicentennial celebration. The building pictured is Squire Bishop's Inn, constructed in 1769 on Town House Hill (the Metcalf Road). The inn was used for the first town meeting. Unfortunately, alterations made over the years diminished the historical value of the structure. The much-changed and deteriorated building survived until the 1980s, when it was destroyed.

WINTHROP, LOOKING WEST FROM HINDS HILL, 1900. This photograph and the following one were taken from nearly the same location, allowing for a good comparison. Mount Pisgah is in the background of both.

WINTHROP, LOOKING WEST, 1960. Note the more numerous trees on the hills in the distance. As farming has decreased, many fields have reverted to woods in short order. The same farm and its white buildings, on the west side of Maranacook Lake, are visible in the upper left of both photographs.

OLD HOME WEEK, 1908. The Pennimen house, on Hinds Hill, is festooned with flag and bunting, in keeping with the patriotic nature of such reunions. The people are certainly well turned out for the occasion.

THE REMICK PLACE. Shown *c.* 1900 is the home of Alva Remick. Houses such as this one, built in a Cape Cod style with attached shed and barn, were once more numerous in town, as everyone farmed a little.

THE SAGER PLACE. This house still stands atop Hinds Hill, although today, it is known as Main Street Hill. Hinds Hill has seen rapid development, with Squire Hill Plaza and the opening of the complex that sits between the old Augusta Road and Route 202.

THE WINTER OF 1917. This view shows the large amount of snow that fell in 1917, a time when snow-removal equipment was in its infancy and much shoveling was the rule.

A HOME ON CENTRAL STREET, C. 1900. Family members pose in front of their well-kept home on Central Street. Grandmother stands on the left, dressed in black, next to the parents of the youngsters lined up along the fence.

BOWDOIN STREET, LOOKING EAST FROM MAIN STREET. A late-summer view of shady Bowdoin Street gives us a glimpse of the trolley going along its way. This attractive picture puts mud season, during which travel along such dirt roads was difficult, out of mind.

BOWDOIN STREET, LOOKING WEST FROM MAIN STREET. The Norcross house is seen on the right in this photograph, taken during the time of World War I. The trees have not grown back to their former beauty. The buildings on the left of the street are still used, but a bank now occupies the Norcross home site.

MAIN STREET, LOOKING EAST. Note the child beside the watering trough. A number of watering troughs were located throughout the town, set out in memory of Dr. J.B. Fillebrown in 1896. Fillebrown was a successful dentist and politician in the 19th century. On the left is the L.T. Carlton home.

THE CONGREGATIONAL PARSONAGE. This was the home of Harry Stevens before it became the Congregational parsonage. The building was later torn down. The Congregational church is now located at the corner of Main and Bowdoin Streets.

THE WINTHROP COMMUNITY HOSPITAL. Located at the corner of Bowdoin and Summer Streets, this hospital was used for medical purposes during the 1920s. It was later converted into a residence by C.P. Gale.

THE WATER CURE. Also known as the Stanley House, this Elm Street establishment treated various maladies with a balanced diet and a lot of pure water. The capacity of this facility is hinted at by its size. The Stanleys are a local family with industrial antecedents who created a large business now known as Stanley Tool.

BOWDOIN STREET, LOOKING NORTH FROM MAIN STREET. The trolley ran along Bowdoin Street past the Congregational church, on the left, and Winthrop High School, in the center. The school was moved to that building from Main Street in 1910, when the Society of Friends moved to its new church in Winthrop center. Today, the building is used a Masonic temple.

BOWDOIN STREET, FROM MAIN STREET, 1970. The trolley tracks have been gone since 1928, and pavement has taken the place of the dirt road. Here, as elsewhere in Winthrop, the trees are making a comeback.

41

THE CORNER OF ELM AND SUMMER STREETS, C. 1900. The absence of trolley tracks indicates that this photograph was taken before 1902. The house pictured at the corner of Elm and Summer Streets belonged to the Davis family. Today, it is the Carriage House Bakery.

THE ROBERTS FUNERAL HOME. The three-generation undertaking business was started in this building by Leon Roberts in the 1930s. The Roberts family still does business in Winthrop, on Bowdoin Street.

MAIN STREET, LOOKING EAST, THE 1940S. Boys play in the street in front of MacNamara's Diner, which is tucked under the large shade tree on the left. Main Street, on the brink of major changes, still looked much as it had for many years.

AN AERIAL VIEW, LOOKING NORTH. The large building in the foreground is the Bailey oilcloth factory. On the left is the Catholic church, and on the right, the Methodist church. In the background, the smokestack of Wadsworth and Woodman divides the view of Lake Maranacook.

HIGH WATER ON LAKE STREET. Periodically, Winthrop experiences mild flooding. The buildings in the background are in Galeville, and the time of year is late winter or early spring. Note in the background the cleared hill, which today is tree covered.

HIGHLAND AVENUE, LOOKING NORTH, C. 1920. These buildings on the left side of Highland Avenue were taken down to make way for a high school and elementary school. The high school was built in 1965 on the site of the buildings shown at the left.

THE LAST HOUSE ON THE RIGHT, CENTRAL STREET, LOOKING WEST. In its day this was a nice home, built conveniently close to town. The last house on the right side of Central Street, it is shown as it looked before demolition in 1968.

THE BISHOP HOME, CENTRAL STREET, C. 1900. This set of buildings seems to be the townsman's version of a connected Yankee farmhouse in miniature. It is the home of J. Perley Bishop, and the women on the steps are likely Bishop's wife and daughter. The horse and equipage are neatly stored in the barn.

THE NORCROSS HOUSE, MAIN STREET. Once owned by the Norcross family, this house was removed in the 1960s to make way for a bank.

THE 19TH-CENTURY SNOW HOME. The Norcross House, on Main Street, was previously owned by Dr. Albion Snow, who began his practice in Winthrop in 1854. During the time Snow lived in it, the house had an open porch.

DR. ALBION SNOW, C. 1890. Active in professional circles, Dr. Albion Snow was highly respected in Winthrop. He wrote important papers on prevailing diseases, served for many years on the Winthrop School Board, and became a trustee of the Maine Insane Hospital in 1879. He is buried in Maple Cemetery; his grave has the largest stone pillar in the cemetery.

THE HIGHLAND STOCK FARM FOR SALE, 1890. This fine farm was being offered as a "gentleman's" summer or year-round home. Besides the "mansion," there were three large barns and an icehouse. The farm and "eleven Jersey cows, oxen, horse, calves, etc. mowing machines, horse rakes, plows, harrows and ox and horse racks" were to be sold at auction.

GREEN STREET, C. 1900. This late-summer view looks along Green Street toward Lake Maranacook. In this neighborhood, generations of Winthrop youngsters have been raised. Many of these houses are still standing.

GREEN STREET NEIGHBORHOOD. Bordered in the back by Mill Stream and in the front by the road, this Green Street neighborhood holds many precious memories of times past.

A Wall Mural, the 1830s. During the 1830s and 1840s, traveling muralists painted scenes such as this on the interior walls of houses, for those people who wanted to pay for them. Rufus Porter and his nephew are known to have been in Winthrop doing such work. This example is from the house of Capt. Samuel Benjamin, on Main Street. Other murals were recently discovered by contractor Steven Wood in renovating his property on Bowdoin Street.

For Sale on Main Street. The Marble & Granite Works provided high-quality headstones, many examples of which stand in nearby Maple Cemetery. The rock was imported from quarries and finished here after an order was placed.

A Large Elm, Greenwood Avenue. Shown is the trunk of one of the biggest elm trees in Winthrop. The house on the left was once a stop on the local stagecoach line, which served the area before the arrival of the Maine Central Railroad in 1849.

MOSES BAILEY (1817–1882). A quiet and reserved man, Moses Bailey ran his family's oilcloth enterprises and was very successful at it. He married Betsy Jones, and they resided in Baileyville. It is said of Bailey that "his life belongs with the class that makes the world richer and better." He and his brother Charles M. Bailey, also a leading businessman, were devout Quakers. Charles M. Bailey endowed the library that still bears his name.

Three

WINTHROP AT WORK

THE CORN SHOP BOYS, C. 1900. This crew worked in a canning factory called the "Corn Shop." Local farmers had a ready outlet for Maine corn, which was shipped out on the Maine Central Railroad.

THE CORN FACTORY, THE 1930s. This complex of buildings was located on Norcross Point, which, today, is a recreational area. The contemporary town beach is on the left. This view shows that the water level in the lake was once higher than it is now.

THE CORN SHOP GATE, THE 1930s. The dam, shown here with the tender's shed on the right, controlled the water level in the lake in relation to water requirements above and below the dam. The buildings on Norcross Point are long gone, but the little tender's shed still stands. Few people realize its role in what was once a big operation.

BUILDING THE MILK FACTORY, 1905. This view looks southwest across the construction site of the facility that was built to produce condensed milk. The buildings in the background are in Galeville and along Lake Street. Note the cleared fields on the ridge, which runs parallel to Lake Maranacook.

A CREW IN GALEVILLE. Shown are typical early-20th-century working people standing by a barn in Galeville. The man in the center and the man on the left, both wearing ties, appear to be in charge. These 15 people were a small economic unit contributing to a town that had a balance of agriculture and industry.

THE OLD MILK FACTORY, THE 1920S. By 1920, the milk-processing business was well established. This photograph was taken looking east, showing the opposite side of the site pictured at the top of page 57.

THE OLD SHOP, THE 1920S. This old building was more suited to the days hinted at by the wagon in the foreground than to those indicated by the signs for gasoline and oil. Torn down not long after the time depicted here, the shop was replaced by a garage.

BONAFIDE MILLS, C. 1960. This complex was first built by C.M. Bailey and Sons for the manufacture of linoleum. The Baileys sold out to Bonafide, which operated the plant for years before selling it to Progressive Distributors. Progressive used the plant until building its large facility on Route 202.

THE C.M. BAILEY SHOP. Shown is the old C.M. Bailey linoleum and oilcloth works in Winthrop. Originally, the business was in Winthrop Center at Baileyville, but after a fire the operation was moved to town, next to the railroad tracks.

THE BAILEY CREW, C. 1900. Here are the men who worked in the C.M. Bailey factory. The second man from the right is the grandfather of Carl Lindholm, who was over 90 years old when he died in the 1990s.

WADSWORTH AND WOODMAN, 1905. This view looks west past the mill that is at the foot of Lake Maranacook. The mill was built in 1905 with a loan from Harris Woodman's relative C.M. Bailey to manufacture oilcloth. The business had a difficult start. Success came gradually, and the company developed a line of coated fabrics. Later known as Inmont, the business relocated and then ceased to exist in the 1980s.

HARRIS WOODMAN AND FLOYD ANDERSON, THE 1960s. The president of Wadsworth and Woodman, Harris Woodman, on the left, and the plant manager, Floyd Anderson, discuss company matters. Under their leadership, the business did well and employed many area residents over the years.

AN AERIAL VIEW, LOOKING EAST, THE 1960S. This winter view of the town shows the intersection of Main Street and Route 41, or Lake Street. In the upper left is ice-covered Lake Maranacook. To the left of center is the Catholic church, and to the right of center are the Methodist church and the Carlton Mill complex.

MAIN STREET, LOOKING WEST. At ground level the town does not look so densely built. Dave Ketchen's Western Auto occupies the bottom floor of the Pennimen Block, on the right. The Congregational parsonage is visible in the center distance.

Four

WINTHROP LANDMARKS

MacNamara's Diner, Main Street. This little landmark was well known to many residents, as well as to people passing through. The location is hard to beat.

MacNamara's Diner. This small eatery did get crowded at times. Summer was especially busy, with the increased population of summer visitors.

A View of MacNamara's. When full, this small establishment could seat more than 30 people. The food was simple and dependably good. The diner closed, and the business moved into a building on Main Street before relocating on Route 202.

JERRY'S LOG CABIN, MAIN STREET, THE 1940S. Across the street from the fire department was Jerry's Log Cabin. A small operation, Jerry's did a good business for a time.

BABB'S LUNCH, 1942. Situated near the railroad station, this diner was a convenient place to sip coffee and wait for the train. Often, hungry travelers stopped at Babb's before continuing on their journey.

BRADLEY'S STORE. Another small operation that is no more is Bradley's. It served food and also sold convenience items to travelers and sportsmen.

MAIN STREET, LOOKING EAST, 1970. In this more modern view, note the Charcoal House on the left next to the Western Union. The MacNamaras opened the Charcoal House before moving their business to Route 202.

THE FRIENDS CHURCH. From the earliest days, this church in Winthrop Center was the base of the Society of Friends in Winthrop. Moses Bailey and Charles M. Bailey were devout members of the congregation. Moses Bailey was clerk of the meeting for a dozen years, and Charles Bailey was a philanthropist who traveled with a Quaker band that played extensively throughout the local region.

Winthrop High School, Bowdoin Street. Before erecting the Winthrop Center church, the Society of Friends used this building as a church. The high school moved here in 1911. High-school students, as well as some eighth graders, attended classes here until the new high school was built off of Highland Avenue in 1929. This picture was taken sometime after 1911.

Winthrop High School, 1929 to 1965. This building was Winthrop High School until a new high school was built on an adjoining parcel in 1965. Now condemned, the old building is due to be demolished in the near future. The high school that replaced this building has itself been replaced by a new facility.

THE CLASS OF 1933. This class was the first to attend the new high school for four consecutive years. Its members graduated during the Great Depression, went on to fight World War II, and then returned and raised their families. Over the years this class has held periodic reunions. The class album and reunion notes are stored with the town records.

THE CATHOLIC CHURCH AND PAROCHIAL RESIDENCE. Looking north, this view shows the Catholic church, buildings, and priest. The trees look young and well tended. The rectory is in the background.

THE PASTOR AND HIS FLOCK, THE 1920S. The priest addresses attentive parishioners on a sunny summer day. The men have hats in hand, as befits a religious gathering. The building in the background is no longer there; a new rectory now serves the parish, along with St. Francis Parish Hall, built in the 1960s.

THE CONGREGATIONAL CHURCH. Constructed in 1825, this building served the congregation for many years. It was converted to apartments after the congregation built its present church downtown. During the raising of this building, the framing collapsed, killing several workers.

DANIEL CARR (1789–1862). One of the leading lay people in the Congregational Church was Dea. Daniel Carr. He arrived in Winthrop in 1813 and worked as a hatter. In 1820, he opened the first temperance hotel in Maine. A man who put principle over profit, he also was opposed to slavery. Revered for his fairness and integrity, he served as deacon for 19 years.

BOWDOIN STREET, LOOKING NORTH. In this view looking toward Lake Maranacook, the Congregational church is on the left, at the corner of Bowdoin and Main Streets, and the high school is in the distance to the right of center. Note the trolley tracks.

THE METHODIST CHURCH. The Methodist church was built in the 1870s. Remodeled and enlarged over the years, it still serves a growing congregation. This view looks north from what is now the parking lot of Winthrop House of Pizza.

A WATERING TROUGH, C. 1900. Watering troughs were placed at various points throughout town so that thirsty horses could have a drink on Dr. Fillebrown. The troughs were presented to the town in memory of J.B. Fillebrown, a dentist and politician who must have been an animal lover. Over the years many of the troughs had to be removed, as they became obstacles when the roads were widened.

WINTHROP LANDMARKS, THE 1940s. Here, in four images, a postcard shows Winthrop to be a religious town. These old photographs were combined and sold in many local stores as postcards. Summer campers and travelers sent them through the mail to home or friends, and the postcards served to advertise the town.

73

FOUR LANDMARKS, THE 1940S. It was common practice to use differing scales to depict several images on a single postcard. For example, the smallest building, the town hall, is shown here as the largest. Of the four landmarks pictured, only the brick town hall, erected in 1855, survives and is still in use. The town is currently making plans to vacate the building and move into space in the most recently "old" high school.

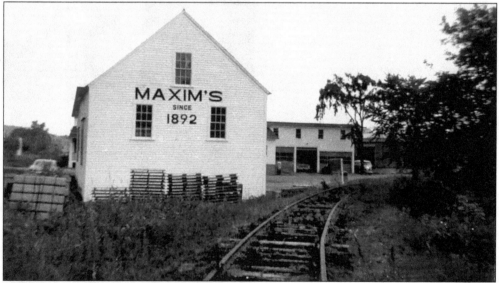

A FAMILIAR WINTHROP NAME. Maxim's Mill ground and shipped grain for many years. In its last days, the business was located near the tracks on Central Street. Chandler Pond Outfitters now occupies the building in the foreground, and Dave's Appliance, owned by the same Dave Ketchen who ran the Western Auto store on Main Street, occupies the buildings in the background.

A BIRD'S-EYE VIEW, LOOKING EAST, C. 1900. This view shows the town be less densely developed than it would be later. The cleared ridges in the background attest to widespread farming at the time. Visible at the far right is St. Francis Church, and to the left of it are the high school and the Methodist church, side by side.

STUDENTS AT THE HOWARD SCHOOL, DISTRICT NO. 5, C. 1890. Winthrop had as many as 12 district schools during the 19th century. Shown are students at the Howard School, built in 1884 in West Winthrop for $941.13. The building was used as a school until 1935.

WINTHROP ELEMENTARY SCHOOL. This school building, constructed in 1952, is on the corner of Highland Avenue and Main Street. Originally consisting of 12 rooms, the school has been enlarged over the years. Current plans call for the elementary school to expand into the vacant high school building.

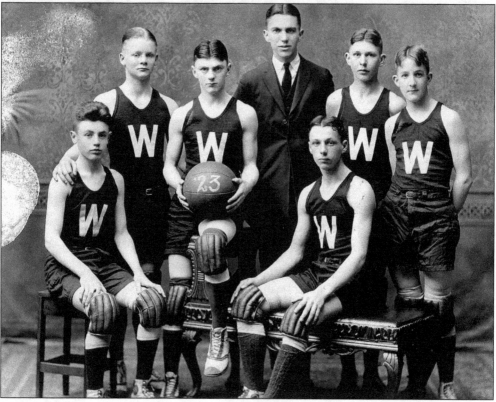

WINTHROP BASKETBALL, 1923. This determined team represented the grammar school for the season. School sports did not exist for youngsters until 1913, and sports programs were not funded until several years later.

THE SEVENTH GRADE, 1919. This photograph was taken in the old grammar school on Main Street. The room has been decorated with pictures considered appropriate for the children's viewing, and someone has spent a considerable amount of time giving the chalkboard its flowery border.

MAIN STREET, LOOKING EAST, C. 1900. This photograph was taken on a sunny winter afternoon in front of what is now the Community Service Telephone Company. It gives a glimpse of how Main Street looked 100 year ago. While many buildings are now gone, Ned's Restaurant and 48 Main Street are still on the north side, and the post office, a tobacco shop, Rheaume's Wear It Again store, and Apple Valley Books are still on the south side.

Five

TRAVEL AND TRANSPORTATION

THE MARANACOOK HOTEL, LAKE MARANACOOK, C. 1940. In the 1870s, the Maine Central Railroad built the Maranacook Lodge on the western shore of the lake. There was a small railroad station named Maranacook. This hotel and others, such as Tallwood on Craig's Point, were also served by steamers plying the lakes.

THE MARANACOOK HOTEL, MAIN LODGE. The well-tended grounds and neat buildings show the Maranacook Hotel in the summer during its peak years. The Maine Central Railroad annually published an informative advertising brochure extolling in print and pictures the recreational opportunities along its line, with Winthrop prominently featured.

MARANACOOK HOTEL GUESTS AND STAFF, C. 1910. In front of the hotel, the happy guests and friendly staff pose for a summer photograph that was later used on a postcard.

MARANACOOK HOTEL GUESTS AND STAFF, JULY 16, 1913. This view appeared on a postcard with the date July 16, 1913. It shows the congenial climate at the Maranacook Hotel during the peak years when it was a summer destination.

THE FLYING EAGLE LODGE, THE 1950S. This name was given to the former Maranacook Hotel by subsequent owners. The Flying Eagle remained open for a few years before it closed forever in the 1960s.

CUTTING AND HAULING ICE FOR MARANACOOK LODGE. The harvesting of ice was an annual winter chore, since large quantities were required for the summer business. Once cut and removed from the water, the blocks were taken to the icehouse and covered with an insulating layer of sawdust. The ice would last the entire summer season. During the 1940s, Purinton Brothers sold ice to any and all.

THE MARANACOOK HOTEL DINING ROOM. The size of the dining room hints at the capacity of the Maranacook Hotel. The shining floors and well-appointed tables denote a first-rate operation that was run with pride.

THE LAKEVIEW HOUSE. A Winthrop landmark, the Lakeview House was a destination hotel. Open for the summer season, it competed with other nearby summer destinations, including the Sir Charles, the Maranacook Lodge and camps, the Belvedere, the Martha Washington Inn, Ponewhush Farm, and Ashaluna Farms. The Lakeview House burned in 1942.

THE WINTHROP HOTEL, THE 1930S. This year-round hotel also housed the IGA grocery store. The two-story building attached to the back of the hotel is now gone, and the dark roof at the far left left is now part of Ralph Calcagni's fitness center.

LAKESHORE CAMPS. After World War II, Maine lakes became more accessible. As a result, many people now own summer camps on lakes in the region. Shown is a powerboat heading north past numerous camps on the east side of Maranacook Lake. The trolley line ran along the eastern shore of the lake; later, the line became the roadbed for Memorial Drive.

THE MARTHA WASHINGTON INN. This photograph shows some of the Martha Washington Inn buildings in the off-season. The guests and staff had separate quarters. The inn was the scene of many happy vacations.

84

HEADING FOR WINTHROP. This steam locomotive was used by the Maine Central Railroad until the 1950s. The railroad then shifted to diesel engines, which it still runs today. An efficient means of travel, steam locomotives hauled thousands of summer people to Winthrop for holidays.

THE MAINE CENTRAL RAILROAD STATION PLATFORM. This view shows the railroad station that served the town until the 1960s.

LAKESHORE TRACKS. Looking toward Winthrop, this view shows the tracks of the Maine Central Railroad running along the shore of Lake Maranacook.

THE MAINE CENTRAL STATION. Gathered at the Winthrop station, people wait for the train. The station agent and his helper stand ready for action, and more than one person is looking to the right toward the arriving train. The Maine Central Railroad had several runs through Winthrop per day, so one could get to Lewiston rather easily.

MARANACOOK SWIMMERS. The town beach is pictured here. Note how close the trolley tracks are to the lake. The trolley tracks and the train tracks ran parallel to each other on opposite sides of Maranacook Lake. From Winthrop, one could make connections to Augusta by means of the trolley system, which lasted until 1928.

THE ANABESSACOOK FLAG STOP AND DEPOT. This small facility served the area south of Winthrop on the Maine Central Railroad's back route from Lewiston. The development of the region as a tourist destination saw small depots, such as this one and the one a few miles north at Maranacook, become very busy places during the summer season.

DOWN AT THE SIDING, C. 1920. The boxcar is empty, and the truck is loaded. The three men with the truck probably have come to help unload the freight. The four women in the boxcar are a mystery, because doing railroad work was generally considered men's work. Perhaps the women are part of a crew from a nearby business and are pitching in to keep costs down.

A DELIVERY TRUCK, C. 1915. This truck is a far cry from delivery trucks in use today. The open cab would have made for rough riding during cold and inclement weather. Small and simple vehicles such as this one helped move America's goods, and as their design improved along with the roads, they helped to send the railroads into an economic decline.

LEAVING WINTHROP ABOARD THE MAINE CENTRAL, THE 1940s. This is the type of train that served the Winthrop region for many years. Tourists came and went on trains, as did hundreds of area men who went off to serve in World War II. For some of Winthrop's World War II soldiers, the last view they ever had of their home was as it disappeared behind the train.

LAKE MARANACOOK, LOOKING SOUTH. Winthrop contains or borders eight lakes and ponds. Before the road system was built, the lakes were used for travel. This photograph was taken from the head of Lake Maranacook.

THE STEAMER AMARRESCOGGIN AT THE WHARF, THE 1890S. This small steamer was run under the direction of Capt. Simeon G. Davis. It hauled passengers, freight, and the mail between the Maranacook wharf in Winthrop to points all over the lake and to Readfield.

CAPT. SIMEON G. DAVIS, C. 1914. A familiar figure around town for over 50 years, Simeon Davis is shown at the wheel of a Ford. Davis came to Winthrop and built the only sawmill that was running in Winthrop in 1890. His mill was on the lower dam, below the Winthrop Mills on Mill Stream. Davis also had a shingle machine. Previously, he had been a cooper on Union Street. In 1880, he put a small steamer on Lake Maranacook, to be followed in 1882 by the *Amarrescoggin*.

A STEAMER ON LAKE MARANACOOK, THE 1890s. A small steamboat is maneuvering near the wharf. Before it can get under way, the operator needs to build a fire in the boiler. In this view looking south, note the inclined ramp running into the icehouse located on the shore of the lake.

BOATING ON LAKE MARANACOOK, C. 1900. The numerous canoes are from the many camps and hotels that dot the shores of Lake Maranacook. Note the steamer lying seemingly still in the water. Everyone appears to have paused while this photograph was being taken.

THE MARANACOOK HOTEL STEAMBOAT STOP, C. 1920. The steamer is stopping either to make a delivery or to pick up passengers. Such boats served the summer tourist business at many resort locations prior to World War II.

DOCKED AT THE ACME. The boat awaits passengers at a lakeside movie theater that also had regulation bowling alleys. A business such as the Acme lived off the summer visitors and the connection to them provided by the steamers—a means of public transportation that no longer exists in the area.

A QUIET DAY ON THE LAKE, C. 1915. The steamers lie at anchor near the town beach. The two cars were probably cut from another picture and glued onto this photograph. In the background are the houses that stood along what is now Route 41, then the road to Readfield and Wayne. Houses are more numerous along that road today. The white house to the left of center above the lake was built *c.* 1800 by Jenness Towle.

THE TOWN WHARF, C. 1900. This rather flimsy wharf was later replaced by a more substantial one. The boat on the right seems to be letting passengers off, while the one on the left, with the crew standing by, waits for a load.

THE END OF AN ERA. A boat moves past the end of Craig's Point. Today, the hulk of a steamer rests in 20 feet of water about 50 yards off of the point. It was burned as a means of disposing of it. Perhaps the wreck is the vessel pictured here. The steamboat days are now long past.

REGATTA DAY, 1957. People still travel under power on Lake Maranacook. Shown at the present town beach are boaters with their speedboats, preparing for a race on the lake.

THE AUGUSTA, WINTHROP, AND GARDINER STREET RAILWAY, 1902 TO 1928. For a time, the local trolley was a popular form of public transportation. It made its last run on August 23, 1928.

PICKING UP A FARE, C. 1910. The trolley awaits customers at Bearce's Camps on Pine Point at Lake Maranacook. The trolley line became the roadbed for Memorial Drive, a street named after a brutal murder in the 1920s.

THE TROLLEY BRIDGE, UPPER DAM, C. 1920. This bridge no longer exists. It was removed in 1929. The present street follows the old trolley line faithfully. Note the horse-drawn grader, on the right, heading north.

THE TROLLEY STOP AND SIDING, PINE POINT. The siding allows one car to pull over to let another pass.

THE CHARLES M. BAILEY LIBRARY. One Winthrop landmark along the trolley line was the Charles M. Bailey Library, located at the corner of Bowdoin and Summer Streets. Charles Bailey was a successful oilcloth manufacturer and philanthropist. Besides endowing the library for the town, he paid to have two buildings constructed at the site of the G.W. Hinckley School. The buildings were named Winthrop and Bailey.

"OLD 108." The trolley known as "Old 108" is shown at the corner of Bowdoin and Summer Streets, across from the C.M. Bailey Library. This picture gives a good idea of what the trolley looked like; unfortunately, most people today do not know what it sounded or smelled like.

LAKE MARANACOOK, LOOKING NORTHWEST, C. 1900. The north end of the lake is in Readfield. The photograph was taken from the western slope, overlooking some lovely apple trees. The islands and the Jesse Lee Methodist Church, in the center background, serve as markers by which to locate this view.

MOUNT PISGAH, C. 1910. This view from the lake shows how far up the slopes of Mount Pisgah farmers worked the land. The buildings in the center are located along modern Route 41. The structure on the shore, to the left of the center, is gone, and the lakeside field has grown up.

WINTHROP, LOOKING NORTH, C. 1960. This aerial view shows Winthrop between the lakes. Route 202, built in the 1950s, cuts across the terrain. The road bypassed the center of town and its stores and shops, and sped travelers along. Note the two settlement lagoons off of Mill Stream, just above Route 202. These were built as part of a pollution abatement plan to clean up Mill Stream and the waters below it.

WINTHROP HIGH SCHOOL, THE 1940s. School is in session in this late summertime view. The old building, scheduled to be razed, will be missed by many. Basketball games used to be played in the building's "Pit," a small space with a tile-on-concrete floor.

Six

STORMS

THE TOWN HALL, LOOKING SOUTH, 1900. This winter view of the town hall was taken before motorized vehicles were in common use. The mill buildings are visible on the right.

MAIN STREET, C. 1900. The winter crew will have to move the deep snow on Main Street before anything else can move. The snow has been pushed alongside the street into banks that are several feet high. A storm in 1888 isolated the town for four days.

A WINTER RIDE, MARCH 10, 1931. From the look of these snow banks, it will be quite a few weeks before the apple trees on either side of the road blossom. It was probably chilly in that rumble seat, but it was faster than walking.

MAIN STREET, THE BLIZZARD OF 1952. These youngsters probably missed a few days of school on account of the storm. They are playing in the snow on the south side of Main Street in front of the old telephone office.

MAIN STREET, THE BLIZZARD OF 1952. On the left, Marsha LaVallee and her sister Virginia stand on top of a snowbank in front of Wilson's Dollar Stores. This was a year of extreme weather that included summer hurricanes.

CENTRAL STREET, LOOKING EAST. The street has not been plowed, but the people are busy scooping the snow. Maxim's Mill is on the left.

CENTRAL STREET, LOOKING WEST. The 1950s and 1960s were quite snowy compared with some recent years. Maxim's is on the right in this view, which is looking toward Galeville.

MAIN STREET, LOOKING WEST, THE 1930S. Three well-togged gents stop to have their picture taken. The sidewalks have been cleared, and the snow has been tossed onto growing banks along the street. In a winter like the one depicted here, the snowbanks grew very high.

STANLEY'S STORE, 1952. Paths had to be dug through the snowbanks to allow patrons to get to the sidewalks that served the stores.

WILSON'S, 1952. This view shows the huge snowbanks resulting from the infamous blizzard of 1952. To remove the snow, town crews loaded it into dump trucks, drove it away, and dumped it elsewhere.

SNOWED IN, 1969. Much digging will have to be done to move the car that is almost completely covered by the snowdrift. This was in the days before many people owned motorized snowblowers, so the old snow shovel was the main tool.

A SNOWPLOW IN TOW, 1952. One of the town dump trucks tries to tow a snowplow past the Winthrop post office. For the blizzard of 1952, the equipment had to be doubled up to make headway on Main Street.

THE BLIZZARD OF FEBRUARY 1969. This storm closed the schools for several days and clogged up the town for a few days as well.

HIGH WATER ON LAKEVIEW AVENUE. This view looking north along Lakeview Avenue shows Frank Horne's garage sitting in the water. Heavy rains and warm weather sometimes combine to raise the water to flood level. The only place to walk without getting wet feet would be along the railroad tracks.

UNION STREET, LOOKING SOUTH, THE 1960S. This winter scene shows the snowbanks under control. From left to right, the buildings are the Morrill Home, Ward's Vacuum Sales, and Andrews Market.

SAND FOR THE STREETS, THE 1960S. The town truck takes a load of sand to a slippery road. Today, plowing and sanding make travel possible in nearly any conditions. Winthrop's excellent highway department works hard to keep roads passable day and night.

THE TORNADO OF 1952. A severe windstorm with cyclonic characteristics roared through Winthrop on July 16, 1952. Nearly buried beneath the birches is Otto Weston's home, on Memorial Drive.

THE TORNADO AT TALLWOOD, LAKE MARANACOOK, 1952. The area around the lake seemed to suffer the most damage. The force of the winds snapped off the tops of nearly all the pines in this young stand.

A DIRECT HIT, 1952. A building at Tallwood was hit and severely damaged by the 1952 tornado. Fortunately, no one was injured.

LAKE MARANACOOK, FROM MEMORIAL DRIVE, 1952. Although the trees have been severely damaged by the tornado, the two camps seem to have survived. The man with the chain saw, in the center, has his work cut out for him; he will need more than one tank of gas.

PROPERTY DAMAGE, 1952. The big pine that has been snapped off lies across the roof of this Memorial Drive property. Although some pines were found to have been hollow-hearted, and thus more susceptible to breaking, many strong and sound trees were broken off with great force as well.

DEVASTATION AT TALLWOOD. The beautiful stand of pines was destroyed nearly to the last tree. The pines that survived are just outside the swath cut by the tornado.

STORM DAMAGE, 1952. Another casualty of the tornado is shown on Memorial Drive. This car was destroyed by a pair of trees that crashed down in the storm. The roar of the winds was deafening, according to witnesses.

DR. L.D. HERRING'S COTTAGE, MEMORIAL DRIVE. This camp and its owner's Cadillac both took direct hits. The car appears somewhat sheltered by the building, which took the full brunt of the trees. Dr. L.D. Herring is using a chain saw on the fallen trees. This can be very dangerous work if electricity is involved and is best left to experts.

DAMAGE IN TOWN, 1952. This view looking north along Route 41 illustrates that the destruction from the tornado was not limited to the lakeshore. Uprooted trees are visible, as is some of the damage done to buildings.

UPROOTED TREES, 1952. The force needed to rip these trees out of the ground is enormous. Only a short distance away, other trees are undamaged. The capriciousness of such weather events is notable.

FALLEN SHADE TREES. The tornado of 1952 was not the only such episode to strike the area. In the late 1990s, a similar but much smaller storm struck; however, the damage was nowhere near that done by the tornado of 1952. Shown are two fallen shade trees waiting for the chain saw to turn them into winter wood.

Seven

PARADES OF THE PAST

THE TROLLEY POWER STATION, EAST WINTHROP. Built in 1903, this brick station still stands in East Winthrop, on land between the old village road and Route 202. For nearly 30 years, it was operated to boost the electrical power used by the trolley.

A HOUSE MOVING, 1908. This picture shows the effort required to move the old ladder factory from East Winthrop up to its present location, where it is now a home. The house on this site burned in 1908, and the unused ladder factory was moved to take its place.

RAYMOND TURGEON, 1945. During World War II, Raymond Turgeon served as a combat engineer in the 90th Infantry Division, which saw action through the end of the war and stayed on as occupation troops. Turgeon, like many of the "greatest generation," interrupted his life and did his duty.

THE TURGEON HOUSE, 1956. Here is the house pictured on page 118, securely sitting on its foundation 48 years after it was moved. It has been the home of the Turgeon family for 53 years.

LIGHTNING OVER COBBOSSEE, LOOKING SOUTH, 1909. This dramatic photograph was taken from East Winthrop village just before a rainstorm that followed much thunder and lightning. It was a lucky shot; the photographer's camera had already been set up, waiting for just such an opportunity.

HENRY PACKARD (1822–1876), EAST WINTHROP. Henry Packard was the 10th of 14 children born to Ebeneezer and Zeruah Packard. A noted farmer, his industry and other excellent qualities were well known. The greatest criticism of him was that "he was a slave to hard work."

GEORGE LONGFELLOW (1813–1895), WINTHROP. George Longfellow was born in 1813. He was raised as a farmer and trained as a teacher. After keeping school for a few years, he took a job traveling nationwide selling Bailey oilcloth during the 1840s. He was a successful businessman and also a noted orchardist, specializing in Longfellow Russet apples, which were famous in New England.

LEVI JONES (1816–1906), WINTHROP. Levi Jones started out as a farmer, became a foreman for the Bailey oilcloth factory, and later ran the whole operation under contract with the Baileys. He was a prominent Quaker, a business leader, and the president of the Winthrop Savings Bank.

OAKES HOWARD (1803–1897), WINTHROP. Oakes Howard was a successful farmer who lived in town. He married Hannah Cobb, and they had six children He served in various town offices and was a founder of the Winthrop Agricultural Society in 1825. He was known as a "scientific" apple grower and a leading orchardist.

MAIN STREET, 1898. The banner hanging across Main Street advertises the election of 1900, when William McKinley sought a second term as U.S. president, with Theodore Roosevelt as his running mate.

THE WINTHROP MILITARY BAND, 1898. Organized in the 1880s, this band was a source of community pride. It was in attendance at patriotic celebrations and parades for many years.

THE WINTHROP MILITARY BAND, 1900. The Winthrop Military Band poses on the steps of the Winthrop Town Hall. Sometimes townspeople stepped in and played with the band, which might have been true of the man second from the left in the back row.

DEDICATING THE CIVIL WAR MONUMENT, 1911. The Winthrop Military Band plays at the dedication of the Civil War monument in 1911. The four men in front of the monument appear to be singing to the assembly, which contained many veterans of "the Great Rebellion" of 1861–1865. The crowd is well dressed for this important day. Although the war had been over for 46 years, the veterans' memories were still fresh. More than 200 men from Winthrop served in the northern forces in the Civil War, 22 of whom died of diseases or were killed in action.

MEMORIAL DAY, C. 1920. A crowd gathers at the town hall on Memorial Day. The presence of an American Legion banner indicates that this view was taken after World War I.

may 30, 1918.

MAY 30, 1918. Returning from a Memorial Day ceremony at Maple Cemetery, the Winthrop Military Band leads the way, followed by a procession of children. When this view looking north along Main Street was taken, World War I was still going on. Today, 85 years later, the Memorial Day celebration and dedication are still held on Main Street and Maple Cemetery is the backdrop for the services.

125

OLD HOME WEEK, 1908. The owners of the buildings from the corner of Main and Union Streets went all out for the celebration. A huge parade was held later, as well as ball games, band concerts, and speeches with patriotic and historical themes.

HERE COMES THE PARADE, THE 1950s. The Winthrop High School Band, led by the drum majorettes, marches east along Main Street.

THE JUNIOR HIGH BAND AND TWIRLERS, THE 1950S. Another year brought another parade on Main Street. While the characters have changed, the annual events still take place. Many residents of Winthrop, past and present, will admit that some of their best memories are of events that occurred right here on Main Street.

FRED RAND AND ROLAND LAVALLEE. Fred Rand, above, is shown shooting some film during the 1971 bicentennial, and Roland LaVallee, left, a Winthrop photographer and friend to all, is pictured with his camera. Winthrop is a better place because of these true sons of the town. This book is dedicated to them, as they are largely responsible for the photographs presented here.